This sawpit at Dalwood, Devon, was built above ground to allow the men to work in more congenial circumstances. To get a tree trunk on to the scaffolding, long inclined timbers had to be erected and the trunk was rolled up them into position (1900).

WOODLAND CRAFTSMEN

Ivan G. Sparkes

Shire Publications Ltd

CONTENTS

Copyright © 1977 by Ivan G. Sparkes. First published 1977; reprinted 1991. Shire Album 25. ISBN 0 85263 381 5. All rights reserved. No part of this publication may be reproduced or transmitted in any form or by any means, electronic or mechanical, including photocopy, recording, or any information storage and retrieval system, without permission in writing from the publishers, Shire Publications Ltd, Cromwell House, Church Street, Princes Risborough, Buckinghamshire HP17 9AJ, UK.

Printed in Great Britain by C. I. Thomas & Sons (Haverfordwest) Ltd, Press Buildings, Merlins Bridge, Haverfordwest, Dyfed SA61 1XF.

COVER: *A besom maker at the Living Crafts Fair, Hatfield House, 1989.*

BELOW: *The tree fellers cutting the birdsmouth or kerf in the front of the tree, indicating the way it is to fall, at Puslinch, South Devon (c. 1890).*

Felled trees whose branches have been removed with a siding-up axe are stacked ready for use by the pit-sawyers, in the Chilterns near High Wycombe (1917).

TREE FELLING

The felling of trees took place traditionally in the autumn and winter months when the sap was down. The craftsmen believed that this provided timber which was more durable and that, in the case of elm, it gave the wood a better colour. The purchaser was allowed a year in which to arrange for its removal. When a *fall* or *stand* of beech was put up for auction, it sold in loads of forty cubic feet, with the number of trees in a load varying in relation to their girth. The trees were selected and marked with a scratcher by the agent to ensure that no mistake was made in the felling.

The *felling axe* in use in England and parts of Europe a hundred years ago had a wedge-shaped iron blade, a straight cutting edge and a long straight handle. During the nineteenth century the *American axe* became popular; it had a curved handle with a bend known as a *fawn foot* in it, also a convex blade and cutting edge made of compressed steel.

Trees from small to medium girth were preferred to large trees for making chair-legs. Sometimes the felling was done by the vender's woodsmen but often the bodgers themselves did it. When a tree was being felled, the first stage was to cut out the swellings or buttresses at the base; this was called *laying up, rounding up, facing up* or *setting up*. Next came the *undercutting*, when the cut known as the *birdsmouth, sink* or *kerf* was made on the front of the tree. Then, with a crosscut saw, the remainder of the trunk was cut from the back of the tree; wedges were driven behind the saw to hold the weight of the tree until it was *thrown* and fell with a crash in the required direction.

After the fall the tree was *snedded, trimmed out* or *headed out*—the side branches were cut away with an axe so that the trunk could be hauled away. Very little waste was allowed in the felling. The *top and lop*, as the smaller branches were called, was trimmed off with a siding-up *axe* and sold for kindling faggots. The mast and brushwood from the beech and oak were gathered to be used as food for pigs.

THE BARKER

The curing of leather used to depend on oak bark, which contains a high percentage of tannin, and on the bark of alder, beech, willow and other forest trees to a lesser degree. As the tannin is contained in the inner or *bast* layers the bark was peeled from the trees in cylindrical sections during April, May and June, when it came away from the trunk more easily.

The bark could be removed either from the felled trunk or even from the standing tree before felling. At the lowest level the first strip of bark was removed by making upper and lower cuts around the trunk with a hatchet, and then the bark was eased off with a *barking iron.* This was a tool in the form of a chisel with a flat round blade which was sharpened around the edge. It was used to make a vertical cut between the two ring cuts. Then the sharpened edge was pushed below the bark and the barking tool was used to lever the bark away from the trunk to remove the section in one piece. Where the bark proved stubborn it was beaten with a mallet to help in its removal.

The stripping was continued on the felled trees down to the branches only one inch in diameter, and smaller barking irons with heart-shaped cutting heads were brought into use.

In some areas the bark could be stripped off the growing tree. Some coppiced oak was grown at eight-foot distances and the bark of each growth was cut about every twenty-four years.

The bark was allowed to dry on low racks or poles and after a few weeks was stored ready for use. The rough outer bark was called *krap* or *ross* and the smaller branches which had been stripped and were to be used as firewood were known as *rendlewood.* The heavier timbers were sawn into lengths to make charcoal and the whole process of barking was commonly called *flawing* or *rinding.*

The cut and dried bark was steeped in water in pits, and the skins to be cured were soaked in this mixture for periods ranging from four to twelve months. Nowadays chemical substances are frequently used in place of bark and, where it is used, foreign barks which have a higher tannin content are introduced.

THE SAWYER

The timber was cut into planks by sawing lengthways along the trunk or sawn crossways into logs to be split or *cleft* by the bodger, the bat maker or other craftsman. The sawing of the tree trunk into planks was a very laborious business and was still done by hand until well into the twentieth century. The men worked over a sawpit, often a permanent construction, as deep as a man's height and up to fifteen feet in length. In the woodland clearings a temporary pit would be dug and two logs were laid along the top with two shorter ones across each end. These logs supported the timber being sawn into planks and were called the *strakes* and the *sills*; iron hooks known as *dogs* were used to fasten the tree trunk to this framework.

The tree trunk was first hewn roughly flat on the upper and lower surfaces to help keep it level. Guide lines for sawing were marked by either charcoal or chalk on the timber with the help of a taut piece of cord. The saw used was a *pit-saw,* which was extremely long, often over seven feet, and which tapered in width from about ten inches at the top to three inches at the bottom. This tapering helped in the movement of the saw and reduced the bottom weight, making it easier for the lower pit-sawyer to return it to the 'up' position. The handles of the saw were detachable, for the blade had to be slid out of each saw-cut or *kerf* as work proceeded across the trunk. The handle at the top which guided the saw was called the *tiller,* while the handle in the pit was termed the *box.*

The saw was steered by the top-man, and it was in the down stroke that the cutting was done. The pit-sawyer underneath was responsible for pushing the blade back up and all the sawdust showered over him. His was a most unhappy task, for, beside the problem of

ABOVE LEFT: *Typical barking iron, although there were several designs. These were made in sets of five or six. The round leaf-shaped head had a chisel edge.* ABOVE RIGHT: *Using the pit-saw. The head of the lower pitman can just be seen under the tree trunk (1908).* BELOW: *Removing the sheet of bark from a felled tree. Note the circular hacket cut around the trunk.*

the sawdust, his view was obscured by the mass of timber above him, and he also had the job of periodically oiling the saw to make it move easily. The plank widths were each cut in turn and sawn one by one outwards from the central cut for a part of the length of the trunk; then the whole trunk was levered forward to allow further sawing. To stop the sawn parts of the tree vibrating, wedges were driven in behind the saw and the end of the trunk was bound tightly with a rope.

This form of sawing continued long after machinery had taken over other functions in the timber trade and the sawpits still exist in the Chiltern woods to remind us of the pit-sawyers at work.

Crosscut sawing was a much easier process than pit-sawing. The tree trunk was cleared of side branches and then rolled up the sloping legs of a pair of *sawing dogs* until they were in the correct position. These dogs were in the form of three-legged trestles and had a long sloping third leg which the trunk was rolled up. Holes were drilled in this leg to take large pegs to hold the trunk in position. The timber was marked with a measure and the two woodmen used the two-handled crosscut saw to cut the logs or *butts* for the use of the chair-leg turner, the cricket-bat maker, the rake maker and the bowl maker.

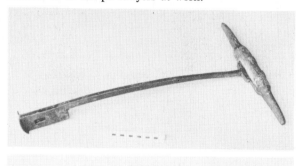

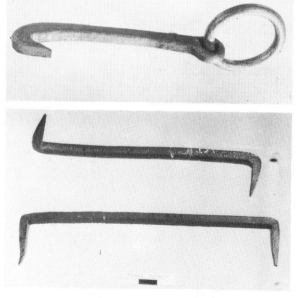

TOP LEFT: The tiller, which was attached to the top of the pit-saw and used to steer the saw along the marked cutting line. CENTRE LEFT: Iron timber dog used to drag timber around the woods. BOTTOM LEFT: The type of iron timber dog used to secure the trunks to the strakes and sills of the sawpit frame. BELOW: This strange frame-saw or pit-saw was used in sawpits. The hands of the lower pitman can just be seen at the foot of the picture.(From 'The Book of English Trades', published in 1827).

6

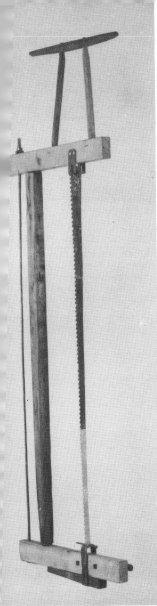

ABOVE: *The felloe saw was used in a sawpit like a normal pit-saw but it had a much thinner blade held rigid in a frame and so could cut curves, such as those required for the felloes of a wheel.* TOP RIGHT: *The box or handle into which the lower end of the pit-saw was fixed, with the two strong handles that enabled the lower pitman to push the saw back into the 'up' position.* RIGHT: *Indoor sawpit showing the iron timber dogs holding the log and the support timbers in position.*

Mark West of Chinnor Hill in the Chilterns finishing the billet on the shavehorse, using the draw-shave, also called the draw-knife.

CHAIRMAKING: THE BODGER

The bodgers employed in the woods worked in pairs, moving to those parts of the forest where the trees stood. When the bodgers bought a stand or fall of trees they would rig up their workshop. At first this was an open hut with sloping sides meeting at the ridge and thatched with brushwood and bracken. The supports were saplings cut to twelve-foot lengths; the end of one was tapered and tapped through a hole cut in the other about ten inches from the top. These were then opened out to stand about twelve feet apart on the ground and the

front and back arches so formed were joined together with side pieces. It was then ready for the brushwood to fill in the sloping sides. In later years, when tools and materials were more likely to be stolen or disturbed, a hut of wood and galvanised iron was used instead, for it could be locked up when the daily stint was completed.

The tree trunks were cut into sections called *butts* with the two-handled crosscut saw. Beech was the popular wood, and the length of the butt varied according to the

OPPOSITE PAGE. TOP: *Using the crosscut saw to cut butts for chair-legs, at Speen, Buckinghamshire (1930).* CENTRE RIGHT: *The crosscut saw with two handles, based on the pit-saw. The right-hand handle was removable.* BOTTOM LEFT: *Splitting the logs with beetle and wedge, and trimming the billet on the high block with side-axe (c. 1908).* BOTTOM RIGHT: *Sawing butts with the crosscut saw. The sawing dog or trestle supports the log, and the peg that holds the log firmly can be clearly seen.*

type of chair-leg being produced. The measure used was known as a *dotter*. The butts were first split in half with either a *beetle* and *wedge* or a beetle and *hand-axe*. The beetle was a barrel-shaped wooden mallet banded each end with a metal ring. It has several other names, such as *bittle, bitel, beddle, commander* or *maul*. The head was often made of apple or elm wood and the handle of ash. The rings were forced on when red-hot, so that they contracted over the beetle head, and they were then securely fixed with spiked nails called *dags*. The half-butts were placed on a flat low block and split into quarters; these in turn were cleft into rough triangular pieces called *billets* with the sharp *splitting-out hatchet*. To prepare the billet for the lathe it had to be trimmed on the high block using a side-axe, which usually had a short angled handle and is ground on one side only. The billets were shaped more closely to a five-sided section and tapered at each end.

The final shaping of the rough billet was done on the *shavehorse,* which was a holding vice with a foot control that clamped the billet in position. The bodger wore a leather apron for safety and using a two-handled draw-knife, or draw-shave as it was often called, shaved the billet clean, ready for the pole-lathe. The bodger sat on the shavehorse and the billet was fixed in the clamp at an angle facing away from him; as he released the foot clamp, so he was able to turn the billet round or over in order to shave another section.

The *pole-lathe* was based on a very ancient principle and it had existed in an almost unchanged form for at least three hundred years up to the late nineteenth century. The pole was the important part: care was taken to choose a young larch or ash tree grown to the right height and thickness. The pole was peeled of its bark and usually allowed to season for a while. To make it more pliable it was shaved on the underside. When ready it was fixed just outside the workshop by a chain attached to a stout post driven into the ground. The other end of the pole was raised and passed through the eaves of the hut and positioned directly over the spot where the lathe was to be set up. A piece of cord would be dropped from the pole to the lathe, wound around the billet set

OPPOSITE PAGE. TOP: *The bodger turning the leg on the pole-lathe. Beside the lathe is a wide range of turnings which have just been completed (c. 1905).* BOTTOM: *The pole-lathe.*

between the poppets and fastened to the foot treadle of the lathe. The billet was fixed between the head and tail stocks, called *poppets,* in which the left-hand side had a fixed mandrel and the right-hand side was adjustable on a screwed iron rod for tightening the work to be turned.

As the treadle was pressed down the cord moved down also, causing the billet to revolve between the poppets of the lathe, and the pole to bend like a bow. When the treadle was released the pole sprang back into its original position, again rotating the billet in the opposite direction. As the motion was speeded up, the bodger was able to shave away the spare wood with a chisel and so shape the chair-leg. First a broad chisel was used to remove the rough surface and create the basic shape; this was called *hogging-down*. The decoration known as the *swells*, the *rings*, the *grooves* and the *beads* were marked with a pointed chisel, and by the use of a few other chisels, such as the half-round chisel and the V-shaped gouge known as a *bruzz, buzz* or *vee parting chisel,* a wide variety of turnings can be achieved.

As well as the chair-legs, the bodger turned the three parts of the stretcher or under-structure of the Windsor chair and also the sticks or rods that support the bow. These sticks were rather thin and tended to whip when in the lathe, so a special support called a *collar* or *bearing rest* was devised to stop this, yet still allow the bodger to turn the stick with little difficulty. The turned chair-legs and stretchers were stacked in the open to dry in the wind. They were then packed into sacks and sent to the nearest chair factory or workshop to be made up. The term *bodger* was applied to the wood turners around High Wycombe and the Chilterns, centre of the Windsor-chair industry in the nineteenth century. A bodger made only the turned parts of the chair; the remainder of the parts and the assembly were completed by the *framer* or *benchman*.

10

ABOVE: *Frame-saw, or dancing Betty, for cutting the curved backstands of the chair.* TOP LEFT: *Chairmaker's side-axe with angled handle. The axe is enclosed in a tool guard.* LEFT UPPER CENTRE: *Chairmaker's draw-shave or draw-knife.* LEFT LOWER CENTRE: *Bow-saw with heavy blade, used to cut the ends of turned chair-legs to size.* BOTTOM LEFT: *The wheel-lathe could continue turning towards the cutting edge of the bodger's tools, an improvement on the forward and backward movement of the pole-lathe.* BELOW: *Beetle, used instead of a mallet in many crafts.*

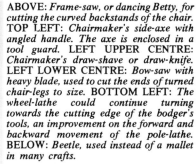

The bottomer at work with the curved and dished adze. Much of the comfort of a good Windsor chair comes from the deep shaping of the seat (1908).

CHAIRMAKING: THE BOTTOMER AND THE FRAMER

The parts of the chair made so laboriously by the bodgers were brought to the factory to be joined to the parts made by other workers. These included the benchman, the bottomer and the framer.

The elm planks cut in the sawpits were fixed to the bench and held rigid with an iron *hold-fast.* They were then sawn into the seat shapes with a *frame-saw.* This was a popular saw with a blade set either in the centre of a square frame or at the side. It was also known as an *up-and-down saw, dancing Betty* or, more unusually, a *Jesus Christ saw.* This name comes from the up and down sawing action for, as the old workmen said, 'you did keep a-bowing to Him.'

The rough seats were next worked by the *bottomer,* who placed them on the floor and, holding each between his feet, used a *chairmaker's adze* to shape the seat. This adze was both curved and saucered; with it the bottomer hacked out the heart of the seat, cutting against the grain to create the comfortable saddle shape for which the Windsor chair is noted.

The next process was making the bow, which is the eye-catching feature of the Windsor chair. A suitable length of ash was boiled in a tank to make it supple and then bent around a *shaping block* and pegged into position until dry. With the use of *spokeshaves* the bow was cleaned and shaved down to shape and the ends were tenoned ready to fit into the arm bow. The splat or decorative panel in the back

of the Windsor chair was cut with a *bow-saw*. The design was drawn from a paper or wooden pattern and holes were drilled with a *spoon-drill*. Into these holes the end of the blade of the bow-saw was threaded and it was fixed back into the bow. The pattern was then cut out as with a fret-saw. The design was tidied up with a series of files.

The framer used a range of traditional home-made tools and worked on a framing block and a sturdy low-level bench. A bench vice was seldom used; instead a tapered wedge and three pegs or cogs were used to hold the chair-legs for marking and boring. The first job was the *legging-up*, in which the holes are drilled in the seat, legs and parts of the stretcher. The drill used had a wooden brace with a spoon-bit, a different brace and bit for

each size of hole, and the set usually hung in a row over the workbench. This lower section of the chair was assembled, glued and forced into position with a *ball-faced turning hammer*.

Once the lower part of the chair had been assembled, the framer had to clean and finish the surfaces. Here a series of spokeshaves, both straight and curved, was brought into use and the final finish was obtained with *scrapers* ground down from pieces of steel, such as broken saw-blades set in a handmade frame. First came the curved blade of the *travisher*, then the *cleaning-off iron* and then the scraper known as a *devil*, with a vertical blade.

The back bow and arm bow were drilled to take the sticks and a mortise was cut in each and in the seat to house the splat.

14

Finally these parts were glued and assembled and the chair was basically complete.

The spoon-drill widely used in chair-making works on the same principle as an apple-corer. To reduce the risk of injury to himself the workman wore, across his chest, a shaped piece of wood called a *breast-bib*. It was attached to his body by leather straps and had a circular recess which the round head of the spoon-drill's brace fitted into.

The chairs were often sent out 'in the white' (unstained) and were called Wycombe whites, but to be stained each part would be dipped into a tank of weak acid to burn in the Venetian red colour which was so popular. One workman recalled doing this task as a child with only sacking to protect his hands and 'crying myself to sleep because of the pain of the acid under my fingernails'. In the eighteenth century many of the chairs were painted, often black or dark green; this both protects the chairs for use outside and hid the fact that they were made with many different types of wood. Nowadays they are mainly machine-made but there are still some firms which, although they use machinery, make them up as individual pieces of furniture and so produce attractive country chairs.

OPPOSITE PAGE. LEFT: *Legging up the chair (1922).* RIGHT: *Cleaning off the seat of the chair with a curved travisher (1922).*

THIS PAGE. LEFT: *The wheelsplat has been cut and the workman cleans and finishes off the design with a wood file (1922).* RIGHT: *Fitting the bow and finishing off the chair (1922).*

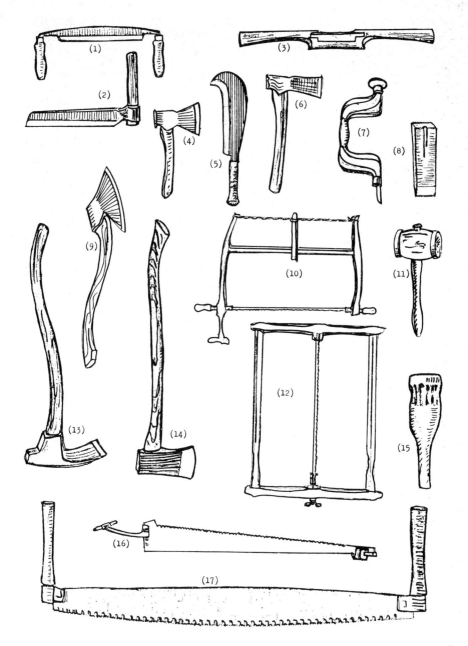

Tools common to most woodland crafts: 1 draw-knife or draw-shave; 2 froe; 3 spokeshave; 4 side-axe; 5 billhook; 6 splitting-out hatchet; 7 brace and spoon-bit; 8 iron wedge; 9 broad axe or siding-up axe; 10 bow-saw with extended handle; 11 beetle; 12 frame-saw; 13 adze; 14 felling axe; 15 froe-club or maul; 16 pit-saw; 17 crosscut saw.

ABOVE: *The stool and the range of tools used in bowl turning.*

THE BOWL TURNER

The bowl turner had much in common with the chair-leg turner, for both worked in the same way with the pole-lathe and depended on the turning chisels for their livelihood. But the type of work and the method of production of bowls varied from place to place; even the woods used and the method of turning might be different.

The general principle was to use tree butts which were similar in diameter to the required bowls, and when the butts had been cut to size the bowl blocks were left to season for six to twelve months. When the craftsman started on the bowl he shaped the outer side of the bowl block into an octagonal section with a side-axe; then he used a draw-knife or gouge until it was a rounded shape. The bowl block was fitted to the head stock of the pole-lathe, which was at shoulder height, and the face of the

block was attached to a special mandrel with four chisel points that held it firmly. This mandrel was then positioned on the point of the tail stock and the cord of the pole-lathe was wound around it as the bowl block itself could not take the drive action.

As the bowl turner pressed the foot treadle so the block turned and with his turning chisels he shaped the outside of the bowl. Then, taking specially shaped gouges and chisels, he cut away the inside, clearing the core of wood until there remained only a thin pillar which was removed by hand with a knife. Then the bowl was polished with beeswax.

In the Berkshire village of Bucklebury Common George Lailey worked for eighty years turning bowls from elm butts, cutting the bowl blocks so that the grain

17

ran across the face of the bowl. The blocks were seasoned for five years before they were ready for use. George was able to cut three or four bowls from one block; each bowl would fit inside the one a size larger. The turning chisels he used, which are now at the Museum of English Rural Life, include many made from old files and of very eccentric shapes. But with them he could expertly cut and separate each bowl from the next, until the nest of bowls was completed.

The bowls were finished at the bench or on a shaping horse with a round support on which the bowl was upturned. Then with his spokeshaves and files he was able to obtain a fine finish in the rosy brown colour and fine grain of elm.

ABOVE LEFT: *William Lailey of Bucklebury, Berkshire, using a hatchet to shape the block into the bowl shape.*

ABOVE RIGHT: *William and G. W. Lailey at the lathe.*

BELOW: *Cutting tools used in bowl turning.*

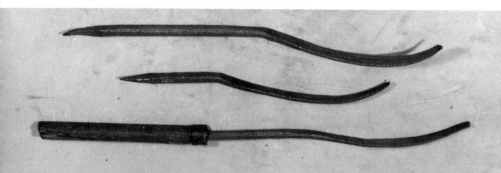

G. W. Lailey cleaning the base of the wooden bowl with a draw-knife.

ABOVE: *A birchwood clogging camp, 1910, showing the pyramids of the roughly cut clog soles and the cloggers with their stock-knives standing by.* BELOW: *The processes of cleaning the clog sole from the rough cleft through to the finished sole.*

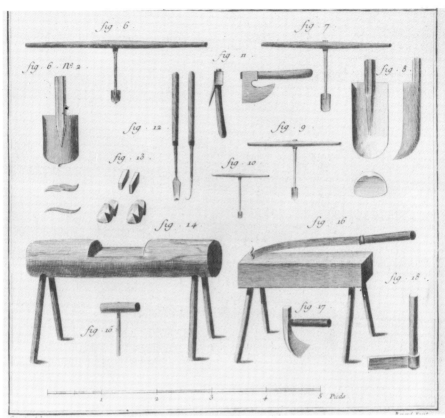

An engraving from 'Agriculture et Economie Rustique' showing the wide range of tools used in the early nineteenth century when clogs were a very common form of footwear.

THE CLOGGER

Clogs were once a very common form of footwear, cheap and durable. They were usually made to a personal pattern and if fitted with an iron rim that could be replaced when worn they would often last for up to twenty years of hard wear. Nowadays their popularity has waned but they are still used in trades in which the workers have to stand for long periods on draining boards or on wet floors, such as in dairy works or farm buildings. They are also worn in such industries as steel and electrical production where they provide extra safety.

The making of clogs was divided between the *clogger,* who made the roughly shaped sole, and the *clog-maker,* who finished the sole, made the leather uppers and fitted the upper and sole together. Cloggers were rural craftsmen working in clogging gangs in the spring and summer and wandering from area to area; they lived in portable huts or shelters made of branchwood and roofed with turf in a similar manner to the huts of bodgers. These gangs worked in Yorkshire, Cumbria, Lancashire, Cheshire and Wales, but seldom in southern England. Dorothy Hartley comments that gypsies monopolised the clog-cutting trade, selling the rough blocks direct to the clog-maker. She adds that sometimes the clog-maker

21

purchased the standing trees and commissioned the gypsies to do the work for him.

The wood used was chiefly alder and sycamore, and timbers with a diameter of between six and eighteen inches could be used. The alder was a particular favourite because of its close-grained wood and, although it is rather soft in normal circumstances, in wet conditions it becomes very durable. Alder can only be cut in spring and summer but the sycamore, which is very similar in nature, can be felled all the year round, so this wood was popular also, especially in Wales, where it is said to be used much more frequently than alder.

The trees were felled and sawn with a *crosscut saw* into logs or butts about twelve to fourteen inches long. These logs were then cleft or split with an *axe* or a *beetle and wedge* into the blocks, which were then trimmed to the rough shape of a clog with the side-axe. This first stage of the process was called *breaking-up.* For the second shaping stage the tool known as a *stock-knife* was used. This had a knife edge about thirteen inches by four inches; at one end of it was a hook which could be slipped into a ring or staple in a bench-top and at the other end was a handle which was often up to two feet in length to give good leverage. This knife, also known as a *bench* or *paring knife*, was used in a chopping motion on the edge and faces of the rough block, paring it to the rounded shape of the clog and cutting the deep notch which forms the instep. Clog soles were often made in pairs and bound together with cord or a strip of leather. The paring and cutting was done while the timber was still green from the felling and the clog soles, or *writhings*, were then stacked in pyramids with sufficient gaps between them to allow the wind to blow through and dry them out.

From this stage the clog became the work of the village or workshop clog-maker. The clogs were usually made to measure and paper patterns were used for the sizes. The rough soles, once dried, had to be finished according to these patterns and the stock-knife was used once again in the shaping process. The upper surface, which had to fit the shape of the foot, was cleaned with the *hollowing knife,* a similar instrument to the stock-knife but with a convex blade about three inches wide. Next the *morticing knife,* also called *gripper-bit* or *gripping knife*, was used to cut the groove around the edge of the sole to hold the leather upper in position. This knife was of a type similar to the stock-knife but had a V-shaped blade which cut the groove. During these finishing processes the clog was supported in the pit of the bench in a wooden frame protected by a leather rest, and the final smoothness of the clog sole was achieved by using various rasps and short-bladed knives.

The leather uppers were also made to pattern, and the clog irons which protected the sole from wear were fitted to the sole and heel with a *clogging hammer.* These irons were specially made to provide rock, that is the curve necessary for comfortable walking.

Finally the uppers were pulled into position with *lasting pincers* and a strip of leather called the welt was nailed around the sole to join the upper to the wood, after the holes had been pierced with a sharp-pointed awl. Flat-headed nails were used and it was important to ensure they went in point downwards, directed away from the wearer's foot.

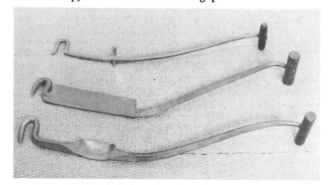

The bench-knives used in making clogs: (from the top) grip or morticing knife; stock-knife; hollowing knife.

The processes in making a cricket bat: (bottom left) the rough cleft; (bottom centre) the shaped blade with the V-shaped cut made for inserting the handle; (top) the parts that make up the handle; (right) the completed cricket bat.

THE CRICKET-BAT MAKER

A particular type of willow, *Salix alba* or the white willow, is used almost exclusively in making the bat blade, and the growing of trees specially suitable for this purpose is an art in itself. The cuttings are rooted at a nursery and are ready for transplant when they have grown as a single shoot nine feet high. These are planted thirty feet apart and are then known as *sets*. The tree grows naturally above the height of nine feet but buds which shoot below this are rubbed off and no branches are allowed to grow which might damage the straightness of the grain. Up to sixteen years' growth is necessary to produce

suitable timber, which is cut at any time of the year it is required.

The trunk was sawn with a *crosscut saw* into three lengths of twenty-eight inches, the standard working length, and this was called a *round*. The round was split with a *wedge* and hammer (or *beetle*) into wedge-shaped billets known as *clefts*. The timber must be knot-free and each cut must be four and a half inches wide at the outer round surface; about eight such clefts could be cut from each round. One firm in Suffolk uses a hundred thousand clefts of willow a year, so it can be seen that a large amount of timber is required. Before the

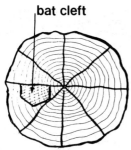

bat cleft

ABOVE: *The section of the billet showing the position of the cleft to be cut for the cricket-bat blade.*

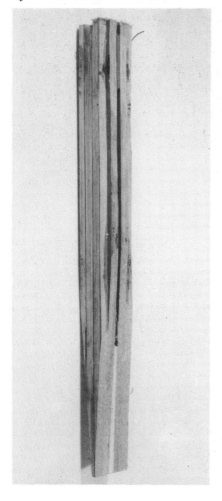

round was split, the shape of the ends of the clefts was marked on the sawn surface. Each cleft was cut so that the face of the bat blade lay on the radius of the round with the annular grain spread evenly as dark lines across its surface.

The wedge-shaped clefts were cleaned of bark, trimmed roughly to shape with a *side-axe* and then stacked in open piles to season out of doors for between nine months and one year. Nowadays they are machine-sawn to shape and graded; then the ends of the clefts are dipped into wax to reduce splitting during the seasoning. This seasoning is done under controlled temperatures and in such a short time that only about eight weeks may elapse between the felling of the tree and the completion of the cricket bat.

The grading eliminated those clefts with blemished uneven grain, knots or discoloration. Following the seasoning, the clefts were cut down to blade size with the *draw-knife,* the *plane* and the *spokeshave* and then forced through rollers to compress the wood. This action made the cricket-bat blade firmer and helped it resist dents from contact with the ball. The shoulders were turned, the *blade* or *pod* was shaped with a hand-axe to its exact shape and a wedge-shaped cut was made to hold the handle.

The bat handle is made from sections of cane glued together into a sandwich with layers of rubber between the sections. The normal arrangement is four sections of cane with three of rubber but in the past as many as fourteen pieces of cane have been used. The handle was sawn to shape, the wedge was cut to match that of the bat and then glued, and the final shape of the handle was obtained with the draw-knife and sander.

Some cricket bats are sold untreated, others highly treated. Many of the hand-tool techniques which made cricket-bat making originally a rural craft have disappeared, with modern bandsaws and jig and spingle moulders speeding the process considerably. But the initial cutting and seasoning still follow the original pattern, for the cricket bat has changed very little in its basic design over the last fifty years.

LEFT: *The cricket-bat handle showing the sandwich of wooden laths and rubber.*

Ernest Sims of Pamber End, Hampshire, straightening the rake handle in the setting brake.

THE RAKE MAKER

With the mechanisation of farming techniques the use of hand tools has declined rapidly, and among the trades that are disappearing as a consequence is that of the rake maker. The hay-rake was made in various parts of Britain and the design varied according to the area. On the sloping hills of Glamorgan a rake with a head which tilted at an angle of forty-five degrees to the handle was traditional; in the fields of northern and western England a rake with a short springy handle was popular, while in southern England a long-handled rake was necessary to cope with the different conditions.

The timbers used include ash, which was the most popular, birch, alder and willow. The rake was made in three parts: firstly the handle or *stail*, then the *rake head*, and then the teeth or *tines*. The stail was made from an ash pole, often stacked

to season for a year with a strip of bark cut off down its length to facilitate the process. The poles were then stripped of the remaining bark and trimmed roughly with a *side-axe*. The pole was usually steamed and straightened in a *setting brake*, a post with two stout pegs or supports between which the pole could be levered straight. In Wales an ash plank was often cut with a bandsaw into strips about six feet long by three inches square; this offered a neat section which was rounded into a pole by the use of a small *rounding plane*. When a rough ash pole was used it had to be shaved with a *draw-knife* in a *shaving brake*. The stails were now rounded and tapered with the *stail-engine*. This was a two-handled cutting tool which had a hole in the centre fitted with a blade, rather on the principle of a pencil sharpener. When the rough stail was inserted in the hole the

ABOVE LEFT: *Shaping the rake head with a side-axe.*
ABOVE RIGHT: *Using the side-axe to chop the butt into billets for making the tines or teeth of the rake.*

stail-engine was worked in a circular motion by moving down the handle and the blade rounded the stail as the action proceeded.

One end of the stail was split or sawn for a length of about twenty inches and a piece of metal or leather was nailed around the wood at this point to stop it splitting further. The split section was then spread into a V shape to be fixed to and to support the rake head. In some parts of Britain the stail was not split but inserted direct into a hole in the centre of the rake head, and two half-moon bows were fitted through two holes in the stail and then inserted into holes drilled into the rake head each side of the stail hole.

The rake head was made of cleft or sawn ash or willow and was about thirty inches long. It was then shaped with a short-handed *broad axe* or a *side-axe* and smoothed to a satisfactory finish with a draw-knife. Holes were bored for the V-shaped end of the stail and a further set of holes, no more than three inches apart, was bored for the tines. The arms of the handle were now driven into the two holes in the rake head and secured with screws.

The butt being used for making the tines was cleft into billets with either a side-axe or a small *bench-knife* before being shaped by the *tine-former*. This was a six-inch length of iron piping about half an inch in diameter and sharpened at one end to a cutting edge. It was fixed on to the *driving stool* (or *tining horse*) over a hole in the stool. As the first roughly shaped peg was forced through it with a mallet the next one was inserted on top and pushed it into the basket below. About fifteen tines

26

were needed for each rake; they were driven into the holes bored in the rake head and their upper ends were sharpened with a draw-knife. Some rake makers used a tine-former which was very similar to a dowel-plate, just a metal plate mounted on a piece of wood, with holes the same diameter as the tines drilled through the plate and the wood support. The partly shaped billets were simply driven through the holes with a mallet and so the round shape was achieved.

TOP RIGHT: *Fitting the tines into the rake head.*
CENTRE RIGHT: *The stail-engine, which acts like a giant pencil sharpener and rounds the ash pole into a smooth rounded handle.*
BELOW: *Joining the stail and the rake head by forcing the two separate branches of the stail into the holes in the rake head.*

ABOVE: *Wiring the brush on the broom-horse. The wire comes up the slope on the broom-horse and is released or halted by a pedal.* BELOW: *The end of the brush is chopped square with a side-axe.*

Cleaning the besom handle or tail with a half-round draw-shave.

THE BESOM MAKER

While the demand for most woodland products has declined, the besom is still popular and much used in the garden and for sweeping the yard. The broom or brush part was made from brushwood, often cut from the crowns of coppiced trees, made into faggots and stacked under cover until required. The bundles were built up into stacks some fourteen feet high with the brushwood laid alternately lengthways and crossways. They were left for several months until the twigs were hard and pliable and then sorted out ready for use.

A bundle of brushwood was bent double to make the main core of the brush and some birch brushwood was added around the outer parts to thicken it out; the whole was then bound tightly by two rings of wire some four to six inches apart. To do the binding the besom maker sat on a *broom-horse* with a foot-controlled wire-clamp, and a piece of the wire was inserted into the centre of the brush about four inches down from the bent end. The besom maker then rolled the brush towards him, catching up the brushwood in the loop of wire as he did so. Then he pressed the foot pedal on the broom-horse and locked the wire. This allowed him to cut the wire and fasten it firmly, keeping the brushwood secure. Another ring of wire was fastened round the brush several inches lower down and the process was repeated. Some besom makers also used an *iron grip* to compress the brushwood before wiring. The bent end of the brush was chopped square with an axe. A *bond poker* was often used to thread the binding material.

The handles, or *tails* as they are called, were made of hazel, ash or lime rods. Any knots were cleaned off, the bark was removed and the rod was smoothed down with a *draw-knife* or half-round *draw-shave*. One end was sharpened to a point with a *side-axe* and then forced into the centre of the brush to a position below the two rings. It was secured by a peg or nail driven through the brush between the rings.

Other materials used in making the brush included ling and marram grass, and the original binding materials such as withy or split ash could be used instead of the wire.

Trimming the end of the besom handle to a point with a side-axe.

Joining the tail with the brush to complete the besom.

FURTHER READING

Bailey, J. *The Village Wheelwright and Carpenter,* Shire, 1975; reprinted 1989.
Blandford, P. W. *Country Craft Tools.* David and Charles, 1974
Hartley, D. *Made in England.* Eyre Methuen, fourth edition 1974.
Manners, J. E. *Country Crafts Today.* David and Charles, 1974.
Mayes, L. J. *History of Chairmaking in High Wycombe.* Routledge, 1960.
Salaman, R. A. *Dictionary of Tools used in the Woodworking and Allied Trades c.1700-1970.* Allen and Unwin, 1975.
Sparkes, I. G. *The English Country Chair.* Spur Books, 1973.
Sparkes, I. G. *English Windsor Chairs.* Shire, 1981; reprinted 1989.
Walker, P. *Woodworking Tools.* Shire, 1980; reprinted 1988.

ACKNOWLEDGEMENTS

The author is pleased to record his thanks to the following: Dr S. B. Ward, Research Officer at the Institute of Agricultural History, Museum of English Rural Life, Reading; the staff of the High Wycombe Central Library. Photographs are acknowledged as follows: Cadbury Lamb, cover; Museum of English Rural Life, Reading, pages 1, 2, 5 (top left and bottom), 6 (all), 7 (all), 8 (centre and bottom right), 11 (bottom), 12 (all), 17, 18 (all), 19, 20 (both), 21, 22, 23, 24, 25, 26 (both), 27 (both), 28 (both), 29, 30, 31; E. Sweetland, pages 3, 5 (top right), 8 (top and bottom left), 11 (top), 13, 14 (both), 15 (both); Sport and General Press Agency Ltd, page 9.

PLACES TO VISIT

Beamish: North of England Open Air Museum, Beamish, Stanley, County Durham DH9 0RG. Telephone: 0207 231811.

Bewdley Museum, The Shambles, Load Street, Bewdley, Worcestershire DY12 2AE. Telephone: 0299 403573.

Bicton Park (James Countryside Museum), East Budleigh, Budleigh Salterton, Devon EX9 7DP. Telephone: 0395 68465.

Blackgang Sawmill and St Catherine's Quay, Blackgang, near Ventnor, Isle of Wight PO38 2HN. Telephone: 0983 730330.

Bridewell Museum of Norwich Trades and Industries, Bridewell Alley, Norwich, Norfolk NR2 1AQ. Telephone: 0603 667228.

Elvaston Working Estate Museum, Elvaston Castle, Borrowash Road, Elvaston, Derby DE7 3EP. Telephone: 0332 573799.

Folk Museum of West Yorkshire, Shibden Hall, Halifax, West Yorkshire HX3 6XG. Telephone: 0422 352246.

Museum of East Anglian Life, Abbots Hall, Stowmarket, Suffolk IP14 1DL. Telephone: 0449 612229.

Museum of English Rural Life, The University, Whiteknights, Reading, Berkshire RG6 2AG. Telephone: 0734 318660.

Museum of St Albans (Salaman Collection of Tools), Hatfield Road, St Albans, Hertfordshire AL1 3RR. Telephone: 0727 56679

Oxfordshire County Museum, Fletcher's House, Woodstock, Oxfordshire OX7 1SN. Telephone: 0993 811456.

Rutland County Museum, Catmos Street, Oakham, Rutland, Leicestershire LE15 6HW. Telephone: 0572 723654.

Ryedale Folk Museum, Hutton-le-Hole, Yorkshire YO6 6UA. Telephone: 07515 367.

Stockwood Craft Museum and Gardens, Stockwood Park, Farley Hill, Luton, Bedfordshire LU1 4BH. Telephone: 0582 38714.

Weald and Downland Open Air Museum, Singleton, Chichester, West Sussex PO18 0EU. Telephone: 024363 348.

Welsh Folk Museum, St Fagans, Cardiff, South Glamorgan CF5 6XB. Telephone: 0222 569441.

The Woodland Heritage Museum, The Woodland Park, Brokerswood, Westbury, Wiltshire BA13 4EH. Telephone: 0373 823880.

Wycombe Local History and Chair Museum, Castle Hill House, Priory Avenue, High Wycombe, Buckinghamshire HP11 2DX. Telephone: 0494 23879.